# Magic Everywhere!

# Magic Everywhere

## How to Do Absolutely Incredible Magic with Totally Ordinary Things

## MATTHEW J. COSTELLO

### ILLUSTRATIONS
### BY GLENN CHADBOURNE

Three Rivers Press/New York

Published by Three Rivers Press, 201 East 50th Street, New York, New York 10022. Member of the Crown Publishing Group.

Random House, Inc. New York, Toronto, London, Sydney, Auckland www.randomhouse.com

THREE RIVERS PRESS is a registered trademark of Random House, Inc.

Printed in the United States of America

DESIGN BY SUSAN MAKSUTA

Library of Congress Cataloging-in-Publication Data
Costello, Matthew J.
Magic everywhere!:how to do absolutely incredible magic with totally ordinary things/Matthew J. Costello; illustrations by Glenn Chadbourne.—1st ed.
Includes index.
1. Magic tricks.   I. Title.
GV1547.C72      1999
793.8—dc21           98-40677

ISBN: 0-609-80357-3

10  9  8  7  6  5  4  3  2  1

First Edition

**TO MY THREE CHILDREN,**
Devon, Nora, and Chris, who remind me
what real magic is . . .
and that it is everywhere!

# TABLE OF CONTENTS

# ACKNOWLEDGMENTS

Thanks to PJ Dempsey, my editor, who saw the magic in the idea. Thanks, too, to my wife, Ann, and children, Devon, Nora, and Chris, who patiently let me practice tricks on them. Glenn Chadbourne's illustrations made these tricks come to life. And Rick Hautala was supportive of the project from the beginning. May all your rabbits disappear to be replaced by shiny coins.

# BEFORE THE MAGIC...

I know. You can't *wait* to do some real magic!

With this book, you can do it with things you find right in your own home. But before you try even *one* trick, I have to tell you some very special, very secret things about magic.

Everything you're about to learn is for you and you alone.

You see, by buying this book, you've taken the first step into the wonderful world of magicians. But that world is also a world of secrets.

Only magicians know these important secrets.

And now you will too!

Are you ready to see yourself *transformed* into a magician?

## Being a Magician

Being a magician, even one who does magic just for fun, is a very special thing. Magicians know more than just how to do the tricks. They also know . . . the Magician's Code. The Magician's Code has time-honored rules that all magicians follow when they perform. If you want to do real magic, you'll remember them.

And they're very easy to remember because there are only two rules!

# The Magician's Code

*First,* never, ever repeat a trick when you perform it in front of an audience!

After you do one trick, follow it with another, saying, "Now, here's something different" . . . or special . . . or even more amazing.

But why wouldn't you perform the trick over?

That might be obvious. If the magician (that's you!) does the trick again, your friend (that's the person or the audience watching) gets to look at things he didn't notice before.

Most of the great tricks depend on your friend's not looking where you don't want him to. So if you do the trick again, you give him a chance to discover the secret.

Which brings us to the second rule of the Magician's Code (and I bet you can guess this one).

*Second,* never, ever tell anyone *how* you did a trick. Your friends will beg you to tell them. They'll say, "Please, we have to know how you did that!" Maybe you'll even think that it might be fun to show them.

It isn't.

Don't even think about doing it.

Want to know why?

When you do a great trick, you've done something really special. You made something "impossible" happen. Or so it seems. And your friends are left amazed.

But . . . you didn't really make the impossible happen, now did you? You distracted your friends, or did something without their seeing, or your friends were tricked into not thinking about something, right?

In other words, magic has a lot to do with things that people didn't see, or notice, or think about.

If you show them how to do the trick, and then show them what they missed, well, they won't be amazed. Uh-uh. Mostly, they'll feel disappointed.

Want to hear what they'll say?

Most likely they'll say something like, "Is that all it is?"

Good-bye, amazement. And you're not much of a magician anymore.

Also, by telling people, you can ruin the trick for other magicians who might do it. If everyone knows how the trick is done, it's not much of a trick anymore, is it?

Now I bet you're wondering how I can tell you. Well, for one magician to teach *another* magician a secret is okay. That's how great tricks get passed on.

By buying this book and working on the tricks, you've taken the first step toward becoming a magician.

You've only started and there's a world of magic ahead of you. Now that you know the secret Magician's Code, you're ready to learn some very cool tricks. All the tricks in this book use easily found objects, from a deck of cards to coins to toothpicks. The tricks are all rated for difficulty from one hat (♣), the easiest, to three hats (♣ ♣ ♣), the more difficult. And don't worry—sometimes the easiest tricks are the best.

Anybody around?

Ready to get to work?

Then let's make magic *everywhere!*

# One

## Ten Really Incredible Card Tricks

*W*hy does every magician do card tricks?

Well, that's an easy one to figure out. After all, everyone has a deck of cards, so what you need to do the trick is always pretty handy.

But there's another secret reason.

Doing tricks that look incredible, almost *impossible,* with an ordinary deck of cards is easy. You won't have to practice for hours to do tricks that look amazing.

Here are a few pointers, though. Always practice your card trick a few times before you try it on a friend. Never repeat the trick and, of course, never tell anyone how you did it.

Here's the first amazing trick, the Floating Cards.

# 1

# THE FLOATING CARDS

*What You Need:* a deck of cards

**RATING:** 🎩

## The Illusion

You deal the top two cards from the deck . . . revealing the red 5 of hearts and the red 6 of diamonds. You point out the two *red* cards, the 5 and the 6, to your friend.

Now you scoop up those cards and stick them in the middle of the deck.

You shake the deck, saying, "I'm making those cards float to the top again!"

Then you flip the two top cards over, revealing the red 5 and the red 6.

Pretty amazing, huh?

## Performing the Trick

Well, this trick's not so amazing when you know how to perform it.

First, you prepare the deck by putting the red 5 of *diamonds* and the red 6 of *hearts* on the top of the deck. Then just below that, you put the red 5 of *hearts* and the red 6 of *diamonds*. That's all you have to do.

To perform the trick, you turn over the top two cards, saying, "See the two red cards, the five and six." Then you stick them in the middle of the deck.

You tap the deck for magical effect and turn over the next two cards. Your friend sees the red 5 and the red 6 . . . and thinks they're the same two cards.

It's an incredible card trick—and so easy!

## Behind the Magic

This trick works because you don't say, "See the red five of diamonds."

You point out the red 5 and 6 without pointing out *what* suit they are. When the next two cards are turned over, your friend thinks that they're the same.

# 2
# THE MAGICAL ACE

## What You Need: a deck of cards

## RATING:

## The Illusion

Ask your friend to deal out some cards, face down, one at a time onto a neat pile. Tell her that she can stop anytime. When she's done, she has two piles—the cards she dealt out and the rest of the deck. Now go get a sealed envelope.

You ask your friend to pick up the pile she made and look at the bottom card. She sees the ace of diamonds. Give her the sealed envelope. She opens it to see that you have drawn a picture of that card—the ace of diamonds!

## Performing the Trick

Before you do the trick, take the ace of diamonds and put it at the bottom of the deck. Now take an envelope and put a drawing of the "magical" ace of diamonds inside. Seal the envelope and put it aside.

When you're ready for the trick, hand the deck of cards to your friend. You could even shuffle the cards first if you take care that the ace always remains on the bottom.

Now here comes the tricky part. Ask your friend to start dealing the cards. Tell her she can stop whenever she wants. Ask her to make two neat piles with the dealt cards in one pile and the rest of the deck in the other pile. Take the pile with the ace of diamonds on the bottom and put it *cross-ways* on the other pile (sort of like a *T*).

Now go get the envelope with your secret prediction. You are set to carry out the effect. Tell your friend to take the top pile and look at the card she cut to. (This really isn't the card she cut to—but she won't know that!)

She will look and see . . . the ace of diamonds.

Ask her to open the envelope—and she will see your drawing of the magical ace of diamonds!

## Behind the Magic

The trick works because your friend *thinks* that she cut to that card, the ace. It's even more amazing if you did a shuffle first—taking care to keep the ace on the bottom.

Your friend knows that she made two piles but doesn't quite remember which pile is which! Trust me, it *is* confusing.

When you ask her to take the first pile and examine the card she cut to, she will believe that's the card she dealt to.

Remember, people will believe you, and that fact is a magician's best friend.

# 3

# THE VANISHING CARD

*What You Need: a deck of cards*

RATING:

## The Illusion

Show your friend three cards: the 3 of hearts, the 2 of hearts, and the ace (1) of hearts. Then place all three cards face down on the table. You ask your friend to pick out the ace of hearts—but it has disappeared!

And in its place is the ace of diamonds.

## Performing the Trick

The trick with this trick . . . is that there *never was* an ace of hearts.

You showed your friend what he *thought* was the ace of hearts.

But the ace was between the other two cards. When you show all three cards, make sure that only the top edge of the card is visible. That way, you can show that it's an ace without revealing that it's a diamond.

When you ask your friend to pick out the ace, he'll assume that it's also a heart. And when he flips it over, he'll be totally surprised to see that it has been changed into a diamond.

## Behind the Magic

This is another trick that works because of what people assume.

In this case, though your friend never sees what suit the middle card is, he assumes it's the same suit as the others. Why should he think otherwise?

And once he thinks that, he will continue to think that right up to the time he flips the ace over and sees that the card he thought was there has vanished!

# 4
# FINDING A CARD WITH A PULSE

*What You Need: a deck of cards*

RATING: ♟ ♟

## The Illusion

You shuffle the deck of cards and then fan them out in front of your friend. Your friend selects a card, then replaces it in the deck.

You ask your friend to cut the deck, then turn the deck of cards over, face up. You say you'll pick her card by holding her finger and feeling her pulse!

You take her finger, move it over the face-up cards, . . . stop at her card, and push her finger onto it.

And you say, "See, I felt it in your finger!"

## Performing the Trick

First, shuffle the cards in front of your friend, then fan the cards out, face down. Ask your friend to take one. Now here comes the tricky part . . .

When your friend takes her card, she splits the deck in half. Take the top half as if you're just waiting for her to put the card back on the bottom half. But when you do, look at and remember the bottom card—your "key" card.

Ask your friend to replace her card while you put the top of the deck on. Now your *key* card is next to her card.

Ask your friend to cut the cards as much as she wants—it doesn't matter. Your key card will always be next to her card. Her card will always be to the *right* of your key card—no matter who many times she cuts the deck.

To finish the trick, spread the cards out, face up. Hold your friend's finger and guide it over the pile. Say, "I will feel your pulse beat faster as you get close to your card." Remember that her card is to the *right* of yours. For fun, pass her card so she thinks you missed it! Then bring her finger back and press it onto the card she picked.

## Behind the Magic

You might wonder why your friend doesn't see you looking at that bottom card. Well, that's because she's *distracted,* looking at her card. Besides, why would she think that your looking at some other card could help find her card?

Then, when she cuts the deck, she believes that her card is well mixed up in the pile. And it is . . . except that your key card, the one on the bottom of that top pile, is always there, to the left of her card.

# 5
# THE GUILTY CARD

*What You Need: a deck of cards*

*RATING:* ♟ ♟ ♟

## The Illusion

This amazing trick requires a bit of tricky card play with the cards held behind your back . . . but it produces an amazing effect.

You ask your friend to take any card from the deck. He looks at it, then puts it back in the deck. You move the cards behind your back for a moment and say to him, "Your card is flipping over inside the deck." When you bring the deck back, you fan the deck with the backs facing up, and one card—his card!—is face up.

## Performing the Trick

Remember, when your friend looks at his card, you can do something that he doesn't see. In this trick, have your friend take a card from the deck.

While he looks at it, bring the deck behind your back and turn the bottom card upside down. Then flip the whole deck

around and bring it back out, so the bottom is now on top.

Again, he's busy looking at his card and, besides, what could it matter what you do with the deck?

When you bring the deck in front again, the bottom card is now on top, showing its back side. All the other cards are face up.

Ask your friend to slip his card inside the deck. Since all the cards are face up except for the top one, your friend's card will be face down.

Move the deck behind your back. Say, "Your card is flipping over inside the deck." Flip that top card over again. Now, there is only one card not like the others—your friend's card!

Bring the deck out front, back facing up. Slowly fan the cards to show your amazed friend one card, his card, face up!

## Behind the Magic

When you flip the bottom card over and then flip the deck, it makes the deck all face up except for that top card. Your friend won't be suspicious about the deck. It's his card he wants you to find—and that's in his hand, right?

But when he slips his card back into the deck, it will be face down in a pile of face-up cards. When you bring the deck around (and his card supposedly flips over), you simply reverse that top card so only one card is not like the others.

Practice this one a lot before you do it—it's one of the best.

# 6

# THE MOST AMAZING CARD TRICK OF THEM ALL

*What You Need: a deck of cards*

**RATING:** 🎩 🎩 🎩

## The Illusion

A friend shuffles a deck of cards, then secretly picks one card. The deck is given back to you—and you pick out the mystery card. It's an amazing effect, but first there are some things you need to do ahead of time. . . .

## Performing the Trick

This special card trick is truly amazing—but you must do some preparation before performing the illusion.

Place any 11 cards on top of the deck, face down. They can be any cards at all except clubs. Underneath those cards, arrange all the clubs in order, from the ace (1) through the

2, down to the king, a total of 13 clubs. Place the rest of the cards underneath the clubs—and you're set! Now you're ready to perform the trick!

**1.** Ask a friend to take the deck of cards and cut them into three piles. Each pile should have about one-third of the deck. Don't worry—it doesn't have to be exact. See the illustrations below.

| Piles | A | B | C |
|---|---|---|---|
| | middle | bottom | top |
| | third | third | third |

**2.** You should have three piles: the middle third of the deck (A) on your left, the bottom third (B) in the middle, and the top third (C) to your right. Now this is important: Remember which pile is which!

**3.** Ask your friend to pick up pile A (the middle third of the deck) and look at the top card.

**4.** After your friend has looked at that card, ask her to put it back on top and then shuffle each pile. That way she *knows* all the cards are really mixed up.

**5.** When all three piles have been shuffled, ask your friend to put pile B (the bottom third) on top of pile C (the top third), then to place pile A on top of the whole deck. You will have to practice this a few times. You don't want to confuse this part!

**A**
MIDDLE

**B**
BOTTOM

**C**
TOP

**6.** Now things get mysterious: Take the deck and ask your friend to concentrate really hard on what her card was.

**7.** Start dealing 17 cards from the top, one at a time. Spread them out . . . the mystery card is coming to you. Now here's the secret: Look for the lowest club, a 6 of clubs, for example. Point to that lowest club (the 6 of clubs) and announce, "This is your card." And it will be!

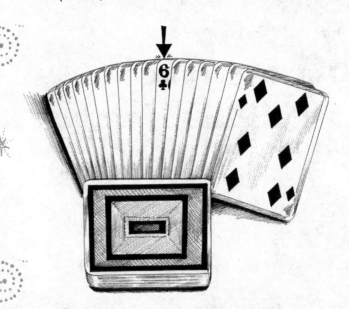

## Behind the Magic

So what makes this incredible trick work?

Well, remember the 13 clubs all in order? When your friend takes the top card from middle pile (A), the top card will always be the lowest club in that pile. The other few clubs are in pile C.

When all three piles are out back together, the A pile, with its clubs, is on top. The other clubs in pile C are on the bottom. You'll *always* know that the *lowest* club in first 17 cards on the top of the deck is the mystery card.

# 7
# THE KEY CARD
## What You Need: a deck of cards
## RATING:

## The Illusion

Here's a trick that is *very* easy to do but seems really amazing. And it will continue to be if you can keep the secret.

You ask your friend to take a card from the deck, any card at all. Then you ask your friend to put his card on top of the deck. Ask him to cut the deck as many times as he wants. Then you turn the deck over . . . and pick out his card!

## Performing the Trick

I said it was easy and it is! It's another card trick that makes use of a "key" card. Here's how to do it:

Before you begin, shuffle the deck a couple of times. This will look as though you're mixing up the cards really well. Except when you've done the last shuffle, look at that bottom card, your key card. Fan the cards and ask your friend to take one and look at it.

Now, you ask your friend to put his card on top of the

deck and cut the deck. Then, when he cuts the deck and places the bottom pile on top, your key card will be right above his card. He can cut the deck as many times as he wants—those two cards will always be together.

Now for the effect . . .

You turn the deck over, face up, and look for your key card. Your friend's card will be to the right of the key card.

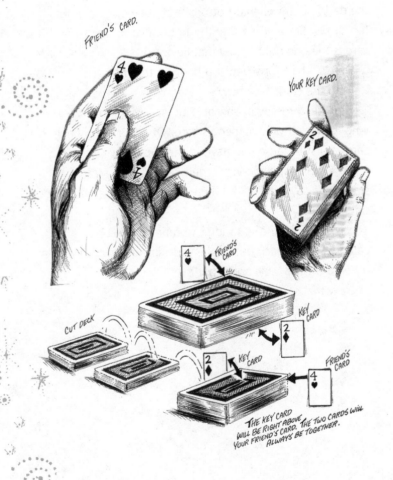

FRIEND'S CARD.

YOUR KEY CARD.

FRIEND'S CARD

KEY CARD

CUT DECK

KEY CARD

FRIEND'S CARD

THE KEY CARD WILL BE RIGHT ABOVE YOUR FRIEND'S CARD. THE TWO CARDS WILL ALWAYS BE TOGETHER.

And if he somehow cuts to the key card, putting it on the bottom of the deck, his card is right on top.

# Behind the Magic

Well, let's think about this a second.

The next card after the bottom card is always . . . the top card. When your friend puts his card on top and then cuts the deck, he moves that bottom card, the key card, right on top of his. Since you *know* the bottom card, you know his card is the one right below that key card.

Here's a hint for when you perform the trick.

Hold the cards face down.

Flip the cards over one at a time, saying you will stop when you get to your friend's card. Of course, you pass his card at first because you haven't seen your key card yet.

So keep flipping, even when see your key card. Then stop—and say you just got a message from one of the cards on the table.

Say, "I'm feeling a strange vibration from one of those cards." Slowly reach out—take your time—and finally pluck his card off the table and flip it over!

Now that's magic!

# THE TRICKY JACKS

*What You Need: a deck of cards*

*RATING:* 🎩 🎩 🎩

## The Illusion

You ask your friend to divide a deck of cards into four piles. Then you ask her to deal out cards from each pile onto the other piles.

But when you ask her to flip over the top card on each pile, she'll see that a "Tricky Jack" has somehow made its way to the top of *each pile!*

## Performing the Trick

This is a great trick, really mystifying when you take the time to practice it.

First, you have to set the deck up by taking out the four jacks and putting them on the top of the deck.

Ask your friend to take the deck and make four piles, from their right to left. (The one with the four jacks on top will be on the right, the *fourth* pile.)

Now ask her to pick up the first pile. Tell her to take the

top 3 cards off the top of the pile and put them on the bottom. (Why? Wait and see!) Ask her to deal 1 card from that pile to the top of each of the other three piles.

Ask your friend to do the same thing with the second pile, the third, and finally the fourth, the one with the jacks on top.

Now tell her to flip over the top card on each pile . . . revealing a Tricky Jack on top of each.

# Behind the Magic

When you ask your friend to pick up each pile and put 3 cards on the bottom, that doesn't do *anything* at all—until your friend gets to the last pile.

Here's why. She picks up the first pile and puts the 3 top cards on the bottom. It doesn't matter what cards at all! When your friend deals a card on top of each pile, she also puts a card on top of—gasp—the the four jacks.

Your friend does the same thing with the second and third piles, putting 2 more cards on top of the jacks!

But now, when you get to the fourth pile, something very cool happens. First, as she did with the other piles, your friend takes the top 3 cards, which were covering those tricky jacks, and puts them on the bottom. Bye-bye, and they are gone.

Now your friend will deal 1 card on top of each of the other three piles. You know what those cards are, don't you? They're the Tricky Jacks, and when your friend looks, she'll find a jack on top of each pile!

# THE ANSWER IS ON YOUR COMPUTER

*What You Need: a deck of cards and a computer*

**RATING:**

## The Illusion

This trick requires some moves with your hand, but nothing you can't practice—and the illusion is well worth it!

You ask your friend to shuffle a deck of cards. You tell your friend that you want him to look at the top card, then put it back anywhere in the deck. He can even shuffle the deck again.

Then you take the deck from him and look for his card. But each card you pick isn't his card!

Some trick, huh?

But then you say, "Maybe it's on my computer."

You go to the computer, turn on the monitor, and there in big letters . . . is his card!

## Performing the Trick

The key to doing this trick is that your friend isn't really picking a card at all!

Before you do the trick, place a card, say the king of hearts, on top of the deck. Go to your computer and use a paint program, if you have one, to write "King of Hearts" in big, bold letters, or maybe draw the card!

You're set to do the trick. Hold the deck behind your back, with both hands behind your back, and tell your friend you want him to shuffle the deck of cards. But before you pass him the deck, slide the top card (the king of hearts) off the top of the deck and hold it in your free hand.

Your friend shuffles the deck and then you ask him to give it back to you.

Put the deck behind your back as you did before. And now slide the king of hearts *back* on top. Tell your friend to pick the top card and you will read his mind to guess it.

Hand him the deck and ask him to look at the top card and then replace it anywhere in the deck. He can even shuffle the deck some more before handing it back to you.

Now comes the fun part!

You fan the deck out, face up, and look for his card, but each time you throw a card down, it's wrong.

That's when you get a brainstorm!

"Maybe it's on my computer!" you say. Turn on the monitor, revealing the card . . . the king of hearts!

As you predicted, your friend's card was on the computer!

## Behind the Magic

The fun of this trick is using the computer. You could even download a picture of your chosen card from a magic website on the Internet (see pages 151–155) so your friend will really see his card on the screen.

# 10

# THE ENVELOPE PLEASE

*What You Need: a deck of cards*

**RATING:** 🎩 🎩

## The Illusion

This trick depends on some tricky moves. But practice it, and you'll stun your friends.

You ask your friend to take a deck of cards, shuffle it, and then give you back the shuffled deck. You then ask her to examine the top card and put it back in the deck. She can then shuffle the deck some more before returning it to you.

Now comes the magical part . . . you look through the deck, searching for her card. You pick out some card, say a 6 of diamonds, and show it to her. But it's not her card!

"Hmm," you say. "Maybe I wrote the name of your card in this envelope." Give your friend the sealed envelope to open. When she does, she will see that you have written, "I predict that you will select the queen of spades!"

And so she has!

# Performing the Trick

As I mentioned, this trick will require some quick moves with your hand and a little bit of setup. Here's how you do it:

First, secretly write your prediction—"You have picked the queen of spades"—on a piece of paper and stick it in an envelope. Seal the envelope and put it to the side. Now take your deck of cards and put the queen of spades on top. You're ready to do the trick.

Hold the deck of cards behind your back with both hands as you tell your friend that you want her to shuffle the deck.

But as you slip her the deck, slide the top card, the queen of spades, off the top of the deck. Your friend can shuffle as much as she wants to. When she gives you back the shuffled deck, put it behind your back with both hands.

Now slide the queen *back* on top. Tell your friend that you want her to examine the top card, memorize it, then stick it anywhere in the deck and shuffle some more.

Pass her the deck. She examines the top card, returns it to the deck, shuffles the deck, then passes it back to you. You take the deck and begin searching for her card. You can pick any card and show it to her . . . and it's wrong.

Ask her to pick up and open the sealed envelope, which happens to be nearby. To her amazement, she sees your incredible prediction. You named *her* card, the queen of spades, in the sealed envelope.

## Behind the Magic

The secret to this cool trick is moving that top card off the deck in a way that your friend doesn't see or suspect anything. Practice the move so that you move the top card off the deck and pass her the deck very casually. The more you practice it, the more it will seem as if you are just handing over the deck to be shuffled.

Remember that your friend will assume that she has the whole deck, and that she picked the top card of a shuffled deck. She will be amazed when she sees the name of that card in an envelope.

# THE GREAT HOUDINI
## Master of Escape

*T*he greatest performing magician of them all was the phenomenal Harry Houdini. Born Ehrich Weiss in Budapest, Hungary, on April 6, 1874, Houdini's family moved to Wisconsin, where he grew up and dreamed of magic. The son of a rabbi, Ehrich ran away and joined the circus.

He started calling himself "Houdini" after the great French magician Robert Houdin, and he soon started dazzling audiences with amazing "challenges." He was locked, handcuffed, in cells and chests, and even placed himself upside down in a tank of water.

But this master of illusion and escapology defeated them all.

How did Houdini escape all these things? In many cases it was less magic than hard work. To get out of a straitjacket, Houdini would rest one elbow on a hard surface and push. This moved his other arm closer to his head, and finally over it. From there he could work a hand out to start undoing the buckles.

Easier said than done!

Houdini also developed something called the Underwater Escape. He was tied up and tossed in the water, seemingly a dead weight. But as Houdini himself explained, "The key to this effect is the escape artist's swimming ability. The feet must kick back and forth with enough force to get afloat while the hands pull at the knots."

Houdini wrote many books on magic, exposed fake mind readers who claimed to have real powers, and dazzled the world with his escapes and illusions.

# TWO

## BENDING SPOONS, EXPLODING SODA CANS, AND MAGIC CRAYONS

*M*agic with ordinary things is a lot of fun. And the great thing about ordinary things is that they are everywhere. (That's why we call them ordinary!) In this group of illusions, you'll use misdirection and suggestions to create strange effects that actually aren't very strange at all. With misdirection, you point your friend's attention away from what you *don't* want her to see. And "suggestion" is making a suggestion about what your friend thinks she is seeing. Some of these tricks can even get a bit messy—you've been warned!

# 11
# THE EXPLODING CAN

*What You Need: 2 cans of soda, unopened please!*

**RATING:**

## The Illusion

You take two soda cans. It doesn't matter what type, though it's fun if they're the same. You ask your friend to shake one like *crazy*, as much as he wants. This is the fun part. When he finishes shaking the can, ask him to shake it some more!

Now you say that you will open it and nothing will happen . . . because you can magically make the bubble move from the shaken can to the other one, which is just sitting there.

You open the shaken can—and nothing happens!

You pick up the other can and ask your friend to open it— and it explodes all over him.

Won't he love that!

## Performing the Trick

There's nothing special about either can. You ask your friend to pick one and shake it like crazy, then shake it some more.

Then you're ready to open it. Just be sure you wait at least twenty seconds before opening. Say that you will make all the fizzy bubbles move from one can to the other. Say some magic words if you like.

After twenty seconds, you open the can in one quick move. Why quick? If there's any pressure at all, a quick open gets the pressure out fast, without any explosion.

Now for the second part, the can that explodes. Take the second can and hold it close to your friend. In fact, point it at your friend!

Tell him to open this can slowly, even though he knows that it hasn't been shaken.

Tilt it toward him. Tell him, "Be careful, open that can slowly." At the sound of the first pop as the can opens, press harder and soda will shoot toward your friend.

Won't that be fun, huh?

On second thought, maybe you'd better use seltzer or club soda rather than soda.

## Behind the Magic

Here's an amazing, secret fact: The first can—the one shaken like crazy—will, after twenty seconds, be perfectly safe to open. After twenty seconds, most, if not all, of the bubbly pressure that has been built up . . . is gone!

You only have to make sure that you pop it quickly. Pull

on the tab quickly and absolutely nothing will happen.

Now, when you extend the other can toward your friend, you press down on the can slightly with your thumb. This puts pressure on the soda just when there's only a tiny hole for it to shoot out of!

And shoot it does.

You seem to have done the amazing: Made the fizzy bubbles move from one can to the other.

# 12
# THE FLOATING CUP
## What You Need: a foam cup
## RATING: 🎩

## The Illusion

Think you can make a cup float right before someone's eyes?

Sure you can.

You show your friend an ordinary foam cup and then tell her that you will make it float before her very eyes.

Then you wrap your hand around the cup and raise it up. So far, no magic. But then you let the cup go—and it floats in the air while you wiggle your fingers.

It's an amazing illusion . . . and it's so easy.

## Performing the Trick

The trick is so incredibly easy—but you have to do one little bit of preparation. Stick a thumb in the back of the cup to make a hole. When you grab the cup, casually stick your thumb in that hole.

Be sure to keep that side of the cup away from your friend—that way she won't see you stick your thumb in the hole.

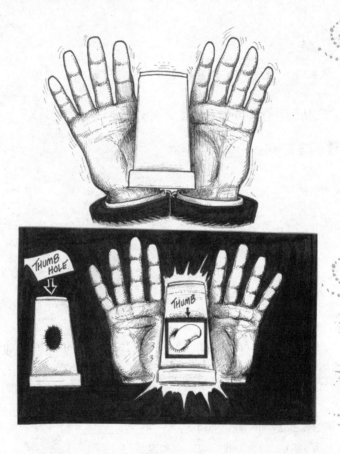

Now, raise the cup before her eyes, holding it in your two hands.

Then comes the magical moment—let go of the cup. Wiggle your fingers. The cup "floats" between your moving fingers.

This is an effect that looks great and all it takes is a little thumbhole!

# Behind the Magic

You won't have to work hard to make this trick work. But there is one thing you might want to add to your magical performance.

If your friend is the type who might be curious, who might want to examine the cup up close, then when you're done making the cup "float," you may want to say, "There's only one way to make this pesky cup stop floating!"

Then take the cup and crush it between your hands.

That way, your friend will never see the telltale thumbhole and your secret will be safe.

# 13

## ALL GONE!

*What You Need:* a coin, a scarf or a cloth napkin, and a rubber band

**RATING:** 🎩 🎩 🎩

## The Illusion

Ask a friend for a coin. You pull out a scarf or a cloth napkin and announce that you will put the coin into the scarf and make it disappear! You take the coin, wrap the scarf around it, and then shake it—and the coin has vanished.

## Performing the Trick

The coin vanishes thanks to a rubber band. Hold the rubber band open between your thumb and fingers. Drape the cloth over your hand and ask for the coin. With your other hand, take the coin and press it into the cloth. Tell your friend that you're doing something magical. Press the coin and some of the cloth in between your fingers. Let the rubber band slide off, encircling the cloth and holding the coin tight.

Now you're ready to wave the scarf.

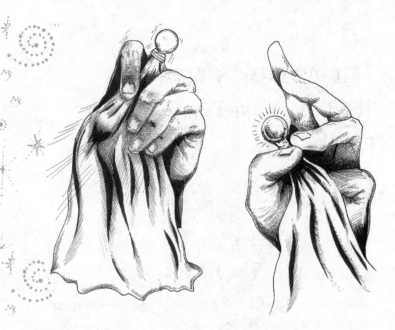

When you shake it, the coin is held by the rubber band. The coin doesn't fall to the ground—it seems to have disappeared!

## Behind the Magic

Practice getting the rubber band set on your fingers so you can stuff the scarf and coin in between the fingers. It will look as if you're pushing the coin into the scarf. Make sure you stuff enough cloth into the "hole" made by your thumb and fingers so that the rubber band holds tight.

And it's important to wave the scarf so your friend sees the side without the rubber band. If the rubber band is tight, you can give the scarf a really good shake and the coin will stay in place, hidden.

# 14
# THE MAGIC CRAYONS
## What You Need: 4 crayons
## RATING: 🎩

## The Illusion

Everyone loves the idea that a magician can see into some-one's mind. In this trick, you pick up the "projection" of a color being sent by a friend.

Here's how you do it:

Put out four crayons in front of you and tell your friend that you will turn away while he picks *one* crayon and puts it into your outstretched hand. You bring this crayon behind your back. Then he removes the other three crayons from sight.

When you look back, there's no way you could possibly know which one he selected and put into your hand.

You ask your friend to think of the color, think hard.

You raise your other hand in front of you, attempting to "see" what color your friend is "beaming" to you.

Your eyes light up . . . you're getting a message . . . and now you announce the color of the crayon still behind your back.

And when you bring your hand out in front and open it, sure enough, there's the color crayon you named.

*THE CRYPTIC CRAYONS*

## Performing the Trick

You do this trick exactly as described above. Your friend selects a crayon and removes the others, and yes—the selected crayon goes behind your back.

But remember the part when you brought your other hand, the one *not* holding the crayon, in front of your eyes? *That* hand tells you what color crayon you're holding behind your back. How could that be?

Here's what you do:

When you have the crayon and both hands behind your back, with your free hand scrape a bit of the crayon top with your thumb. Just a bit . . . just enough so that when you bring that hand in front of your eyes and the thumb is pointing to you, you will clearly see the color of the crayon right under your fingernail.

Easy enough, then, to announce what the color is—astounding your friend!

## Behind the Magic

There are two moves that will make this one of the easiest and most effective illusions you can do. First, when you bring the crayon behind your back, talk to your friend, asking him to think about his color. This banter will cover what you're doing behind your back.

Oh, yes, practice scraping crayons so that you can do it effortlessly.

The second part is harder. When you bring your hand in front of you, move your fingers around in a magical gesture. Make your fingers wiggle while you sneak a quick peek at your thumb.

Practice this one and you'll be a very colorful mind reader!

# 15
# THE AMAZING BENDING SPOON

*What You Need: a metal spoon*

**RATING:** 🎩

## The Illusion

Think you can bend a spoon?

Sure you can! But can you make it perfectly straight by blowing on it?

That's what you do in this terrific illusion. First, you grab an ordinary spoon in your two fists and, pressing forward, bend the spoon. Your friend watches, so far unimpressed. (She can bend spoons too, no doubt.)

But now, you take the bent spoon, blow on it—and suddenly it's straight!

And you're ready for some cereal!

## Performing the Trick

It's easy to make a spoon straight . . . if it's never been bent at all.

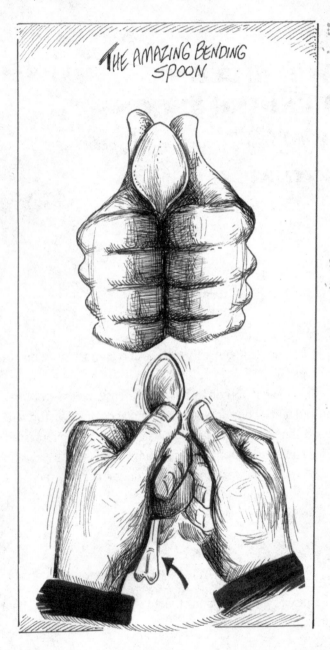

Grab the spoon in both hands, but actually hold the spoon between your index and ring fingers. If you face your friend, it should look as though you are holding the spoon tightly in your fists. But actually the spoon goes through your fists and behind your hand, pointing right at you.

Now comes the performance part of the trick. You *roll* your fists forward as though you're bending the handle part of the spoon forward. It will look as though you are bending the spoon.

When the spoon is "bent," hold it tightly in both hands, covering it. Tell your friend that you will make it unbend by blowing on your hands.

Blow, and slowly uncover the straight spoon.

## Behind the Magic

What we think is happening is always based to a great extent on what we see and hear.

In this trick, your friend sees that you appear to be holding the spoon tightly in your hands when actually the spoon handle sits between your fingers. All you must do to make the "bending" convincing is act as though you're applying pressure to make the spoon bend.

No need to grunt—it is, after all, only a spoon. Just tense up a bit and the impression that you are bending the spoon will be complete.

As will your amazing "straightening" of the spoon!

# 16
# THE LINKING PAPER CLIPS

*What You Need: 2 paper clips and a dollar bill*

**RATING:** 🎩

## The Illusion

Here's a trick where you can see the power of a dollar bill—at least to make two paper clips link without your ever touching them.

Take a dollar bill and fold it in half the long way. Then fold the left third of the bill toward the *right.* Slip a paper clip over the bill to hold it in place. The longer loop of the paper clip should be on top, facing you. Got that?

Now, turn the bill over. Again, fold the bill over to the right and again clip the bill together on this side—but clip only the two top layers. The long end of the new paper clip should also be on top.

Now, simply hold the bill up, grab the two ends of the bill, and pull!

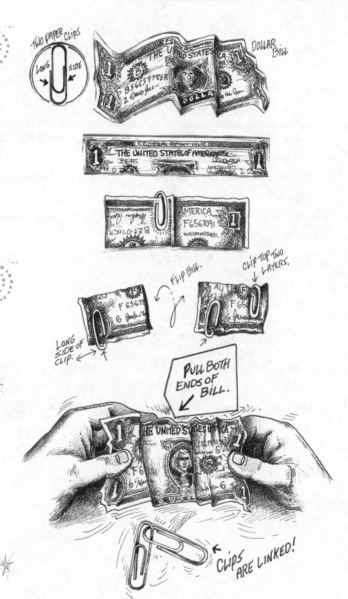

TWO PAPER CLIPS

LONG SIDE

DOLLAR BILL

FLIP BILL.

CLIP TOP TWO LAYERS.

LONG SIDE OF CLIP.

PULL BOTH ENDS OF BILL.

CLIPS ARE LINKED!

The paper clips will fly into the air—and land.

And when the paper clips land, they are joined together!

## Performing the Trick

This is a self-performing trick. Set it up right, and the trick will happen automatically.

And how do you do that setup? The secret is in how you fasten each clip. Make sure the big end of the clip is on top, and that each clip is holding together only two parts of the folded dollar bill.

Now, just by pulling the bill apart, the clips link up, . . . as if by magic.

## Behind the Magic

Take your time practicing this one. Line up the clips, and then practice yanking the bill to make sure it works. You also want to practice pulling the two ends of the bill smoothly so the linked clips really go flying into the air. If you're fast, you can even catch the joined clips in midair!

# 17

# THE HANDKERCHIEF TRICK

*What You Need: a handkerchief or a piece of rope or clothesline 2 to 3 feet long*

**RATING:** 🎩

## The Illusion

Here's a trick that's more of a puzzle than an illusion, something every magician likes to have in his or her routine, something to challenge the audience with.

In this case you lay the handkerchief down as you see in the illustration. Then you challenge your friend to pick up both ends of the hankie or rope and, without letting go, tie them into a knot.

Seems easy, right? But when anyone tries to do it, he fails completely.

But you can do it very easily. . . .

## Performing the Trick

For you to do what seems to be an impossible trick, grab the handkerchief according to the illustration below and then pull it tight.

And presto—you have tied the handkerchief into a knot by grabbing each end and not letting go.

## Behind the Magic

To make this trick more magical, practice grabbing the ends and pulling them quickly. Everyone watching you will miss how it all works.

Needless to say, this is a great trick to do at fancy restaurants with big linen napkins. Let the whole table try to do it before you amaze them.

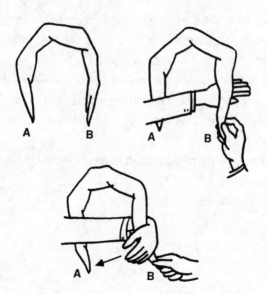

# 18

# THE MAGIC SCARF

## What You Need: a coin and a square handkerchief or scarf

## RATING:

## The Illusion

Can you pass a coin right through a handkerchief or a scarf? Sure you can.

You take a coin and cover it with a scarf. Then tell your friend that you will make the coin pass right through the material. Place the coin in the center of the scarf. Flip the scarf forward so that the coin is completely covered.

Then say some magic words like "Abracadabra" or "Coin-o, Emerge-O."

As your friend watches, you slowly push the coin right through the fabric, before her startled eyes. You can even show her the handkerchief afterward so she sees that it's perfectly fine, no holes anywhere.

So how *does* that coin go through the handkerchief?

# Performing the Trick

Did you figure out the tricky move in this trick?

Here it is. When you put the coin in the center of the scarf, and you flip the scarf forward to cover it, you do something to make sure that the coin *isn't* really covered.

The coin is held between your thumb and forefinger. But you also pinch a bit of the material of the scarf. Then, when you flip the scarf over, the coin looks covered but actually it's not.

You say your magic words and pretend to work the coin through the material until it appears, as if it magically slid through the material.

# Behind the Magic

As with any trick that has a quick, hidden move, this trick should be practiced a lot so that your secret pinch of the material isn't seen and the flip looks perfectly natural. Practice it a lot, and you'll be a pro at making coins pass right through material.

# 19

# THE BROKEN TOOTHPICK

## What You Need: 2 toothpicks and a handkerchief

## RATING:

## The Illusion

You tell your friend that handkerchiefs can do some pretty amazing things. Things like this . . .

Place a toothpick in a handkerchief. Wrap the handkerchief around the toothpick and then *snap* the toothpick in two (with a nice loud snap!).

Then wave the handkerchief in the air—and the toothpick is still in one piece!

## Performing the Trick

Something broke—you heard it—but what?

Before you do the trick, get another toothpick and, making a small hole, slide it into the hem of the handkerchief. Proceed with the trick as described above except when it comes time to break the toothpick. Then, you snap the toothpick that's hidden in the hem.

When you wave the handkerchief in the air, the broken toothpick appears whole!

## Behind the Magic

Here's a good case of using your friend's senses to trick him. He thinks he hears the toothpick being snapped, and he actually does hear a toothpick being snapped—but not the one you put into the cloth.

Will he think you have another one? Not unless you tell him!

# THE INCREDIBLE
# JOHNNY ECK

### And His
### "Saw a Man in Half" Trick

*J*ohnny Eck was a most unusual performer who, early in this century, performed what was one of the most amazing tricks in magic history, called the "Saw a Man in Half" trick.

Here's how the trick worked.

A "magician" called for an audience member to come forward to be sawed in half. A volunteer raised his hand and came up to the stage. Once there, the magician quickly strapped the volunteer into a coffinlike case and then produced a nasty-looking saw. The magician proceeded to saw the case noisily in half.

Then, the sawing competed, the magician opened the case and the volunteer walked out, apparently unharmed.

Everything appeared okay . . . until the volunteer took a few steps and wobbled a bit and the top half of his body fell to the floor. The audience shrieked! But it was not over yet! The top half of the volunteer's torso started moving, the man's face smiling as he scurried away using his arms as legs.

You can can imagine the sound in the theater.

That scurrying torso was the Incredible Johnny Eck. Johnny, born with no legs or lower body, sat on the shoulders of a short person. When the "magician" opened the case after cutting, the short person and Johnny, dressed in a full-length suit, got up and started walking back to the audience until it was time for the upper part of the body to fall to the floor.

Johnny went on to appear in Hollywood films and perform this routine all through the country. Oh, and that original volunteer? That was Johnny's brother, his full-size, normal twin!

# Three

## Mind Reading, Amazing Predictions, and Supernatural Forces

Wouldn't it be great if you could read minds and predict the future? Well, you can. Couldn't be easier.

Thanks to the tricks in this section, you'll be able to perform amazing feats of mind-blowing mentalism and make surefire predictions. I'm reading your mind right now . . . that you're ready for the first trick!

# 20
# THE SEALED PREDICTION

*What You Need:* a business envelope, a piece of paper, and scissors

## RATING:

## The Illusion

Who wouldn't like to predict what team will win a big game?

Here's a simple trick that will have you predicting anything from who will win the Super Bowl to the next World Series champs. And all you need is an envelope, a piece of paper, and scissors.

You say that you will write down who will win a baseball game, for example. Put your prediction in a sealed envelope. When the game is over, you open the envelope and reveal that you correctly predicted the winner!

## Performing the Trick

1. Before performing the trick, cut a piece of paper so it will fit inside your envelope perfectly without folding.

**2.** Now, on the paper, write the prediction like this:

> **The Mets
> Will Be
> The
> Winner
> Will Be
> The Yankees**

Take care to space the words, as shown here.

**3.** Put your prediction in the envelope (remember which team is where!), seal it—and you're ready.

**4.** Announce to your friends that you have predicted the winner of the game and sealed your prediction in this envelope. Put it in plain sight, sit back, and enjoy the game.

**5.** When it's over, and you know who won, go get the envelope and cut it open. If, for example, the Mets won, cut the envelope open at the *bottom*. Let the bottom fall to the floor while you take out the top piece. It should look like this:

**The Mets
Will Be
The
Winner**
------------------------
**Will Be
The Yankees**

The bottom is cut off . . . leaving the amazing prediction above!

6. Of course, if the Yankees win, simply cut off the top, leaving:

**The Mets
Will Be**
------------------------
**The
Winner
Will Be
The Yankees**

## Behind the Magic

As you may have guessed, this nifty trick can be used to predict anything with two outcomes. And no matter what happens, you'll always have correctly predicted the outcome!

# 21

# THE AMAZING MENTALIST

*What You Need: 10 slips of paper and a hat or box*

**RATING:**

## The Illusion

You ask a roomful of friends to shout out the names of *any* ten things in any one category.

Categories could be ice cream flavors, cartoon characters, movie stars, whatever!

As they shout them out, you write them down, one on each piece of paper.

When they're done, you say that you will ask someone to pick a name out of the hat. Then, through the wonders of "amazing mentalism," you will predict what's on the paper.

Sound hard?

Never fear.

A friend takes a slip out, and before she opens it, you say what you *know* to be on it.

She opens it, and there it is . . . exactly the thing you named.

## Performing the Trick

Okay, this trick has a really cheesy secret.

But trust me, if no one knows it or sees it, your friends will be amazed!

When the first person shouts out a name, say, "Donald Duck," you write it down. Now, when the second person shouts out a name, you write . . . "Donald Duck" again. And so on, until you have filled all ten slips of paper with the name Donald Duck.

When your friend comes up to take a slip, any slip at random, you can say with assurance that she has selected . . . Donald Duck!

## Behind the Magic

You see, your trusting friends assume you are writing down each name.

So when you say what's on the selected slip, they will be very surprised indeed.

Here are two pointers, though: You should control the hat or box holding the slips. After your performance, you want to make *very* sure that you casually dump the slips into the garbage, where no one will see them.

# 22

# THE MAGICAL THING

## What You Need: an assistant

## RATING: 🎩

## The Illusion

This illusion requires that you have a partner, a magician's assistant, just like the famous magicians.

You say that you will leave the room while, with your assistant's help, another friend picks an object in the room.

After he has selected the magical object, you return to the room and your assistant names a series of objects found in the room.

You predict that you will select the "magical thing" when your assistant names it.

And amazingly, no matter *what* your friend picks, you are able to predict the selected object every time.

## Performing the Trick

You know . . . one reason that famous magicians use assistants is that assistants can be pretty useful in doing a trick. In this little bit of trickery, you and your assistant have set up a special code.

If, for example, you do this trick in your living room, you would agree ahead of time that your assistant would always name the magical object right after saying, for example, "the rug."

Once your assistant asks, "Is the magical thing . . . the rug?" and you answer "No," you now know, clever you, that the next thing your assistant names—whatever it is—is the selected magical object.

## Behind the Magic

This trick brings the suspicion out in people.

They think that maybe your assistant is winking or shifting on his feet or doing any of a dozen things to let you know when he says the magical object.

That's fine—because you can say, "Go ahead, blindfold my assistant, sit him in a chair, cover him with a blanket."

None of it will matter. The only thing you have to make sure of is that your assistant is told the name of the magical object.

Then you just wait until you hear the "key" word, and you know that the selected magical object will be the next one your assistant names.

# 23

# EASY TELEPATHY!

*What You Need: pencil and paper*

**RATING:** 👤 👤

## The Illusion

Telepathy is the supposed ability to receive thoughts from or send thoughts to others. Some people actually believe that it really exists. Here's an easy mind-reading trick that may make your friends believe that you have telepathy.

You tell your friend that you will ask her some questions and she will come up with a number. As she writes down her answers, you will really *read her mind* to get her answers.

When she's all done, you will have the same number as she does!

First, ask her to write down the year of her birth. You look at her, then write something down. You have telepathy—you're picking up something!

Tell her to add to that year the year of some important event in her life. Again, look at her, thinking hard, and aha!—you write something down.

Tell her to add her age, rounding up if she'll have her next birthday this year (for example, 14½ equals 15). You may know her age, but still you can stare at her, thinking hard before you write.

Finally, tell her to add the number of years since the important event (for example, from 1992 to 1998 would be 6 years). You don't know her "event" or the year, but that doesn't matter. You have easy telepathy, and you write down . . . something.

Tell her to add up her numbers. Offer to give her a calculator.

You don't need a calculator, though, as you write down a number on a piece of paper—and it's her number!

# Performing the Trick

First, when you ask your friend to answer those questions, you can write anything you want. Any number, anything at all—because it doesn't matter.

You simply make sure that you look as though you are thinking magically about the questions, trying to read your friend's mind.

The instructions, in order, are:

- Write down the year of your birth.
- Add to that the year of some important event in your life.
- Add your age, rounding up if your next birthday is this year.
- Add the number of years since the important event.
- Add up your numbers.

Remember, after each question, look as if you're getting a message from "somewhere." When your friend has finished adding her total, you write down a number that is *twice* the current year. (For example, for 1999 it would be 3998.) She will have the same number, every time—and you have telepathy!

# Behind the Magic

When you ask your friend to think about all those numbers, it may seem as if she is picking special, secret numbers and adding them. But remember, in magic *seems* is a powerful word.

Look at what really happens:

She wrote down the year of her birth. Then she added the year of some important event in her life. But then you tell her to add her age, and that brings the first number, the year of her birth, right up to—ta-da—the current year! Right?

When you tell her to add the number of years since the important event, that brings the *second* number up to the current year also. When she totals the numbers, she will of course have twice the current year.

And it will seem amazing!

# 24

# MAGIC TEA

## What You Need: a small card, a pencil, and 2 cups of herbal tea in light-colored cups

## RATING: 🎩

## The Illusion

Here's a trick that may have your friend thinking that you can really see through things. But to better prepare him for the wonders: Fix him some nice herbal tea so that he's better able to appreciate the magic about to happen.

Your friend sits across from you at a table, and both of you have a nice cup of herbal tea. You hand your friend a small card, like an index card, and ask him to write down a series of five numbers.

You look away while he writes, and then ask him to turn the card over. You ask him to pass the card—face down—over to you. When he does, you take it from him and put it, still face down, in front of you.

You look at the card, face down, stare at it, concentrate—then announce the five numbers your friend wrote on the card.

*The numbers will be reversed, like in a mirror image.

Flip it over, and of course you are correct. You can see through the card!

## Performing the Trick

It would be nice if you could see through things, but in the world of magic and illusion, things are not what they seem.

Take this trick, for example. Everything occurs just as described above. Your friend writes down the numbers, he turns the card over, he passes it to you. And the card truly cannot be seen through.

So how do you know the numbers?

Remember the soothing herbal tea? That's key to the trick. When you take the face-down card from your friend and slowly bring it close to you, you pass it *directly* over your teacup. Now, look down. You will see the five numbers reflected in the top of the cup. The top layer of tea acts like a mirror, a mirror only *you* can see.

You place the card face down and, having seen the five numbers, announce the numbers to the amazement of your friend!

## Behind the Magic

I bet you can see what you need to practice with this trick: two things! First, you have to move the card over your teacup smoothly so that your friend doesn't notice you hesitating or hovering over the teacup.

Also, you have to practice reading the numbers upside down since they will be reversed in the teacup. Oh, and don't forget to drink the tea when the trick is done and your friend is still wondering how you did it.

# 25
# MIND-READING DICE

*What You Need: 3 dice*

**RATING:** 🎩 🎩

## The Illusion

You give your friend three dice and tell her that the magic in dice grows when you stack them up.

You then turn away from your friend and tell her to stack the three dice one on top of another, in any order. Then you ask her to add the two touching faces of the middle and top dice.

Then tell her to add the numbers found on the touching faces of the middle and bottom dice.

When she has that, you turn around and tell her to add a last number—the number showing on the bottom face of the bottom die. You quickly turn away.

When she's done, she can cover the dice with a cup so that when you turn around, you can't see anything.

You then write a number down on a sheet of paper and hold it up. And it's her secret total from the magical stack of dice.

4

3

6

1

5

2

ADD NUMBERS,
= 21
SUBTRACT TOP
NUMBER 4.

21
- 4
**17!**

## Performing the Trick

Here's how to do the trick:

Your friend takes the three dice and stacks them together while you look away. As described, you ask her to add the numbers on the two touching faces of the middle and top dice, and then add the numbers on the two touching faces of the middle and bottom dice.

But here's the important part of the trick. When she's finished that adding, you turn around and glance at the top face of the top die. Say it's a 4, for example.

You turn away again and ask her to add the last number

on the bottom face of the bottom die. After she covers the stack, you can turn around . . . and tell her the total.

To get the secret number, subtract the number that you saw on the top die from 21 (in this case $21 - 4 = 17$) and you have the magical number.

## Behind the Magic

Like other tricks involving dice, this one also uses the fact that any two faces opposite each other always add up to 7. So each of the dice's opposite sides in the stack add up to 7. There are *three* dice, so the total of all the sides, from bottom to the top must be . . . 21.

When you turn around to give your last instruction and glance at the top, you are looking at the *one face* that is not added. Subtract that number from 21, and you have your friend's total—and a pretty cool trick!

# 26

# LOCKED-DOOR TELEPATHY

**What You Need:** an envelope, aluminum foil, and 5 "magic symbol cards"

**RATING:** 🎩

## The Illusion

There's no cooler trick than mind reading, and here's a trick that will have you reading minds through a locked door *and* aluminum foil.

First you need five magic symbol cards and someone to play your assistant. The five cards are:

1. a circle
2. a square
3. a star
4. a plus sign (+)
5. wavy lines

You also need aluminum foil and an envelope. Announce to your friend that you and your assistant will perform mind

ENVELOPE

ALUMINUM FOIL

WRAP CARD IN FOIL.

PLACE IN ENVELOPE.

FAR LEFT = ① - THE CIRCLE.

reading using these mystic cards. Then you ask your assistant to step into a closet.

Tell your friend that you want him to point to one card, which you will wrap in aluminum foil. Then you will put the card in an envelope, which you will seal.

Your friend selects a card and you wrap it tightly in the foil, then slip it into the envelope, and then seal the envelope.

You ask your assistant if he is ready to "see" what's in the sealed envelope.

When he says yes, you slide the envelope under the door. He can now touch the envelope for vibrations, but he doesn't take it all the way in.

You say that you are projecting to him an image of the selected card.

Can he see it?

He hesitates a moment—and then announces that the card is . . . exactly the card and symbol chosen by your friend!

## Performing the Trick

Of course your assistant can't "see" the hidden card.

But you know what card you put in there. And you give your assistant a "cue" as to what that card is.

How?

When you slide the card under the door, its position tells him what the card is.

If it's the circle, you slide it under at your extreme left.
If it's the square, slide it slightly left of center.
If it's the star, slide it to the right of center.
If it's the plus sign, slide it to the far right.

What about wavy lines? Slide the envelope in dead center, lengthwise.

Despite all the aluminum foil, your assistant will know what the card is!

## Behind the Magic

A nice touch with this trick is to slide the envelope in only halfway. That way your friend knows your assistant is in a dark closet, can't see anything, and can only touch the envelope.

Then you can slide the envelope out again.

When your assistant announces what the magic symbol is, the envelope will have remained sealed, in front of your friend's amazed eyes.

# 27
# THE MAGIC SIX
## What You Need: 17 cards
## (any playing cards in any order)
## RATING: 🎩

## The Illusion

Deal out the 17 cards to make a "Magic Six" as you see in the illustration. Ask your friend to think of some number larger than seven. But before she tells you that number, say you will predict what card on the Magic Six she will land on using her chosen number.

As soon as she tells you the number, you start at the top and count your way down the spiral and then around, counting out her number. Then you count her number again backwards, but go around the circle instead of out of it.

And when you stop, she can flip the card over and see that you have marked that card, and that card alone, with an X.

## Performing the Trick

Arrange the cards as shown in the illustration and mark an *X* on the card you see that's the 12th card counting from the top.

The trick works by itself, and it always works.

But the question is . . . why?

## Behind the Magic

Remember that you told your friend that her number had to be larger than seven? If you look at the Magic Six you see that once you count down past seven, you are in a circle. And what's one thing we know about a circle?

That if you count one way and then count the other way the same amount (your friend's number) you'll end up in the same place, every time . . . in this case, seven cards into our Magic Six.

# 28
# THE MAGICAL NUMBER
*What You Need:* pencil and paper
## RATING: 🎩

## The Illusion

Using a "force," a magician can get a friend or even a whole audience to do something without their being aware of it. Sound impossible? Actually, people are pretty easy to force. For some reason, we usually don't see it when we're being secretly urged to do, or think, or pick.

Here's a great force that almost never fails . . . and even when it does, there's a way to make it work!

You secretly write down a number on piece of paper, then ask your friend to think of a number. He selects his number, and when he looks on the piece of paper, it's the same number!

## Performing the Trick

1. Before you perform the force, write the number 37 on a piece of paper and put it on the table.

**2.** Say to your friend, in a very mysterious tone of voice:

"I want you to think of a two-digit number between one and fifty. Both digits must be odd, and they must *not* be alike. For instance, you cannot pick eleven." Pause for him to pick a number.

"The number you have selected is . . . coming to me . . . okay, it's . . ."

**3.** Ask your friend to tell you their number.

**4.** Reach down to the table and hand the piece of paper to your friend. He opens it and—amazing—it's his number: 37!

## Behind the Magic

How does this incredible force work?

It sounds as if your friend can pick any two-digit number, doesn't it? But look again at the instructions.

You told your friend: "I want you to think of a two-digit number between one and fifty." Okay, two digits . . . that means only numbers between 10 and 50, so goodbye to 1 through 9. Then you said, "Both digits must be odd." Whoa, that means nothing in the 20s and the 40s (since 2 and 4 are even). Your friend, who wants to get a number, is now left with the 10s and the 30s and the number 50.

But the force continues, as you say: "And they must *not* be alike. For instance, you cannot pick eleven."

This is a big force. Told that he cannot pick 11, your friend quickly jumps to . . . the 20s! But that's no good. He moves on to the 30s, maybe thinking about 33. But—gasp!—that's no good since the two digits cannot be the same!

Panic sets in. And most people breathe a sigh of relief when they get to 37—the exact number *you* wrote down.

But . . . maybe not. Most people will choose 37. But a few will pick 35. And if your friend does, you should have in your pocket another piece of paper with the number 35 on it.

"See," you say, "I still had your number all the time."

One of the great things about this force is that you can do it to a whole room of people at the same time—and you will *make* most of them pick the number you want.

# 29

# STAR POWER

## What You Need: paper, pencil, and a hat

## RATING:

## The Illusion

Think you can sense the star power of a famous movie star? This trick will convince people that you really can.

First hand a sheet of paper to your friend.

Tell her to fold it into thirds the long way. Ask her to write on the top third the name of any person in her family. Then ask her to write the name of any friend of hers on the bottom third. Finally, she should write the name of some really big movie star in the middle third. The bigger the star, the more star power there will be for you to sense.

Now, without your looking, ask her to rip the paper into thirds and put them into the hat.

And you are all ready to sense the star power.

Ask your friend to bring the hat close to you. You reach in and announce that you can already sense the piece of paper with the star's name. You feel around for a second . . . and then bring out the piece of paper—with the movie star's name on it.

## Performing the Trick

The trick is set up exactly as described above. The moment the "magic" occurs is when you reach into the hat. The three pieces of torn paper aren't all the same. Two have one edge ripped while the third, the middle one, has two edges ripped (since it was in the middle).

It's simple for you to feel for the sheet with two rough edges and produce the movie star.

## Behind the Magic

Here's a way you can make a good trick seem even more amazing. Before you give your friend any instructions, ask her to blindfold you. Then there can be absolutely no question of your seeing anything.

But feeling? That's a different story. You can certainly "feel" the star power.

# James Randi's Paranormal Challenge

Can anyone really read minds? Magician James Randi is waiting for proof.

James Randi is a master magician who has performed live and on TV for audiences around the world as "the Amazing Randi." He's also an author, lecturer, amateur archaeologist, and astronomer.

Twenty-five years ago, the Amazing Randi issued a remarkable challenge: He said he would pay $10,000 to anyone for "the performance of any paranormal, occult, or supernatural event, under proper observing conditions." The prize was even increased to $100,000 for a special TV broadcast, "Psychic Powers Live."

To date, the prize money goes unclaimed, and the Amazing Randi's challenge goes unanswered.

Besides writing books and performing on TV, at the White House, and in theaters worldwide, Randi helped found the Committee for the Scientific Investigation of Claims of the Paranormal (CSICOP), an organization devoted to the examination of paranormal, occult, and supernatural claims.

# Four

## Coin Tricks

Why are there so many magic tricks using coins? Well, what does nearly everyone have in his or her pocket? That's right, coins. They're pretty much everywhere.

Here are some great coin tricks that will have you doing everything from guessing what coins a subject has in his pocket to easy sleight-of-hand tricks that will make coins vanish!

# 30
# WHERE DID IT GO?

## What You Need: a coin
## RATING:

## The Illusion

Here's a trick that's so simple, you might think that it can't really work.

You hold up a coin, show it to your friend, and announce that you will make it disappear. Then after you drop it (oops!), you pick up the coin and make it disappear before your friend's eyes. The coin has vanished!

## Performing the Trick

Sometimes, a simple trick requires even more practice than a complicated one. It has to go so smoothly that no one sees the simple trick that makes the illusion work.

You start by holding the coin in your hand and announcing that you will make it disappear. But then, as you hold the coin, it slips from your fingers and falls to the floor. Perhaps your friend laughs at you—after all, that *was* pretty clumsy.

But when you reach down to pick up the coin, you pick

up nothing. Casually slide your shoe onto the coin as you pretend to pick it up.

Now hold up your hand, which you've made into a fist, and announce that you will blow in your fist and make the coin disappear. Your friend waits, and then you blow and open your hand, revealing an empty palm. The coin has vanished.

## Behind the Magic

Why should such a simple trick work? Your friend actually thinks that you've dropped the coin. Maybe you seemed a little nervous, performing a new trick. When you reach down to pick it up, it looks like you're doing just that. You even act a little embarrassed. No one will suspect that you've actually picked up nothing!

But you may have one question.

What do you do with the coin under your shoe? Just wait until your friend turns away, and you can bend down as if tying your shoelaces. Pick up your coin and you're ready to do the trick again.

# 31
# VANISHING COINS
## What You Need: 4 to 6 coins
## RATING: ♣

## The Illusion

Take a pile of coins out of your pocket and hold them in one palm. Show the pile to your friend and then reach over and take one. Put the other coins back while you announce that you will make *that* one disappear.

Hold up your hand with the coin. Count one, two, and three—and make a throwing gesture up to the sky. And absolutely nothing comes flying out of your hand!

## Performing the Trick

This trick is perhaps the easiest trick in the book, but the one you really need to practice. You do exactly what is described above—with one big difference: You don't actually take a coin from the pile of coins.

Instead, you reach into the pile just as though you're taking a coin, but take nothing. You slip the rest of the coins back in your pocket.

Of course, when you open your hand, there will be nothing there.

## Behind the Magic

This trick sounds like it shouldn't work—but it does. The key is practicing reaching for a coin and really taking it. Do it a lot so you really know what it looks like to reach into your palm and take a coin. Then, start practicing the same moves, only this time don't take the coin!

Pretty soon it will look as if you're picking up a coin when you're picking up nothing. And you know—making nothing disappear is quite easy.

# 32
# MULTIPLYING DIMES

What You Need: 5 dimes and double-sided tape

RATING:

## The Illusion

Scatter four dimes on the table and announce that you will turn those four dimes into five.

Slowly, gather the four dimes and slide them close to the edge of the table. You say, "You know, when dimes get together, they multiply."

Of course they do!

Open your other hand to show that it's empty, then put it at the edge of the table to catch the dimes as you slide them over the edge.

You close your first, blow on it, and when you open it, there are five dimes!

## Performing the Trick

Well, sorry! It really isn't that *this* easy to make money.

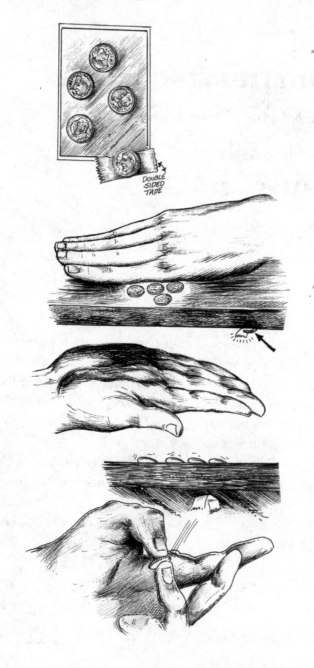

DOUBLE
SIDED
TAPE

But here's how you create the illusion that you can make another dime appear.

Before beginning the trick, put double-sided tape on the fifth dime and stick it under the table right near the edge. As you push the four dimes on the tabletop close to the edge, show that your other hand is empty, ready to catch the dimes.

But when you put your palm under the table, use your fingertips to make the dime taped under the table fall into your hand. At the same time, push the other dimes over the edge.

Close your fist quickly, blow on it, say some additional magic words like "Make-O Money-O!"

When you open your fist, you will have five dimes there.

## Behind the Magic

The secret to this trick is timing!

You want to slide the dimes on the table into your palm *at the same time* as you flick the extra dime into your palm. If all the dimes arrive at the same time, your friend won't notice anything.

One more thing—this trick will work with pennies, quarters, nickels, whatever. But I don't think you can do it with dollars.

Hmmm . . . wait a second. What if you rolled each dollar into a little ball, and did the trick that way?

I'm going to give that a try right now!

# 33

# THE DISSOLVING COIN

What You Need: a coin, a glass
half full of water, a handkerchief,
and a rubber band

## RATING:

## The Illusion

Place a coin inside the handkerchief with one hand. Then hold the coin in position by pinching it under the handkerchief with your other hand.

With your free hand, take the glass of water and drape the coin and handkerchief over the glass. You let the coin fall, your friend hears it land in the glass.

Now you remove the handkerchief and your friend sees the coin in the glass. Re-cover the glass with the handkerchief and ask your friend to fasten the handkerchief with a rubber band at the mouth.

Then put the glass on the table. You announce that you will make the coin disappear!

Clap your hands and then ask your friend to remove the handkerchief—the coin has vanished!

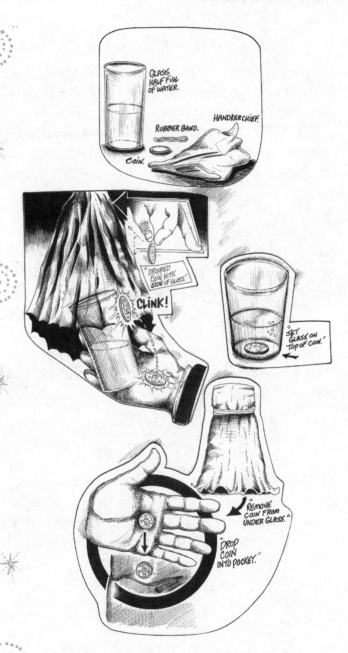

## Performing the Trick

You put the coin in the center of the handkerchief. Then, from under the handkerchief, you pinch the coin to hold it in place. Turn the handkerchief over, with the coin hidden.

Now you're ready to work your magic. You do drop the coin, but you also tilt the glass (see the illustration) so the coin hits the *outside* of the glass. The coin lands in your hand.

Then—before you remove the handkerchief—slide the coin under the glass.

Now, when your friend looks at the glass, the coin *appears* to be on the inside on the bottom. After your friend re-covers the glass and puts the rubber band on its mouth, you close your fingers on the coin as you place the covered glass on the table.

When she takes off the handkerchief, she will see . . . an empty glass. (Make sure to slide the coin into your pocket while your friend uncovers the glass.)

## Behind the Magic

When you drop the coin, it makes a clinking noise. It sounds as if it landed in the glass, so that's what your friend believes.

When you slide the coin *under* the glass, it will look as though it's inside the glass. (Try it—it does.) And your friend did hear it land in the glass, didn't she?

Once she believes it's in the glass, and she covers it with the handkerchief, she won't even think that the coin's hidden in your hand!

# 34

# CRAFTY COINS

*What You Need: a pile of coins*
*(between 12 to 18 coins are fine)*

**RATING:** ♟ ♟ ♟

## The Illusion

You dump a pile of coins in front of your friend. Not to spend, you tell him, but simply to make into three equal piles. He can use as many coins as he likes—as long as there are at least 3 coins in each pile and all the piles are equal.

You ask your friend to call out any number from 1 to 12, and you will make that number of crafty coins appear in the center pile.

You turn around while your friend makes the piles. You then give your friend instructions to move coins from the end piles to the center, and also to remove coins from the center.

Finally you tell him to add a certain number of coins in the center pile.

When you turn around, you see in the center pile exactly the number he had called out.

THIS WILL ALWAYS LEAVE...
NINE COINS IN THE CENTER
PILE.

## Performing the Trick

Sound impossible? Again, this trick depends on what your friend doesn't see. Here's how to do it.

First, as described above, your friend makes the three piles (with at least 3 coins in each pile). He calls out a number—any number—from 1 to 12.

Here's where you confuse him:

You ask him to take *3* coins from each of the end piles and put them in the center. Then he counts the number left in either end pile (it doesn't matter which one—they're both the same).

You ask your friend to remove that number of coins from the center and put them in either end pile. Again, it doesn't matter which.

This will always leave 9 coins in the center. (Try it—you'll see it always works.)

Now, to make the number your friend called out, you can ask him to add some more coins to the center—he tells you how many. And you will be able to tell him his number without seeing a thing! Simply add 9 to that number.

## Behind the Magic

This trick, like so many number and counting tricks, depends on your friend's getting confused. But if you look at the trick you'll see that when you start with three equal piles, your directions always makes the center pile have nine coins.

Your friend won't see how you did it—and that's great.

It's even more mysterious when you create the number they freely selected without seeing any of the piles.

For added magic, do it blindfolded!

# 35

# LEFT OR RIGHT?

*What You Need*: a penny and a dime

**RATING:** 🎩

## The Illusion

Ask your friend to conceal a penny in one fist and a dime in the other without letting you see which hand has which coin.

Then ask her to multiply the coin in her right hand by 6 and the coin in her left hand by 7. She adds those two numbers together and simply tells you whether the answer is odd or even.

And as soon as she tells you, you tell her which hand has the penny and which the dime!

## Performing the Trick

Here's one of those tricks that simply couldn't be easier to perform. If the number your friend gives you is even, then her right hand holds the penny. If the number she tells you is odd, her right hand holds the dime.

# Behind the Magic

The trick works because multiplying the dime by any number will make an even number. So whether it's 7 or 9 (making 70 or 90), it makes absolutely no difference. But multiplying the penny by 6 makes an even number, while multiplying it by 7 makes an odd number. Once you know whether the total is even or odd, you know which is in the right hand, the penny or the dime.

# 36

# SUPER COINS

*What You Need:* a penny, a nickel, and a dime

**RATING:** 🎩 🎩 🎩

## The Illusion

This classic illusion tricks your friend's sense of touch.

Start by asking your friend if he has any coins in his pocket. You're looking for a penny and a dime, you say. And if he happens to be out of spare change, you should have those coins available. (And yes, you need those *exact* coins to do this trick, and the nickel—but more about that later.)

Now you take the dime and place it into the palm of your left hand. With your right hand, you pick up the penny and put it on the tips of the fingers of your left hand. Now you close your fist.

The dime is in the center of your palm, while the penny is held between the thumb and index finger. Bring your hand under the table and tell your friend that this trick must be done without seeing for the magic transformation to occur.

You ask him to reach under the table and take the two

coins from you. He does, feeling the penny and the dime.

Ask him to hand the penny back to you under the table.

You take it from him, leaving him with the dime.

Bring your hand up on the table and announce that you will make the coin in his hand *exchange* places with the coin he just gave you.

Slam your fist down on the table, and there's the dime!

And what does he have?

He *thinks* he had the dime, but when he brings his hand up and looks, he sees he is holding the penny!

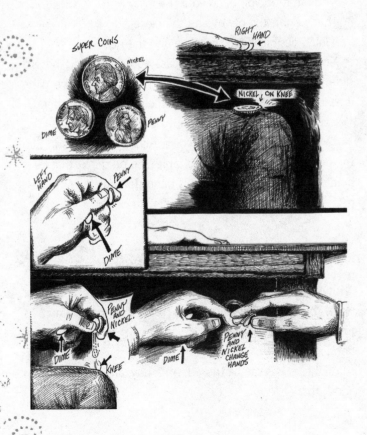

# Performing the Trick

Remember the nickel?

This masterpiece of misdirection requires that you hide that nickel on your knee.

After you palmed the dime and the penny, the dime is in the center of your palm. Magicians call this "palmed" because it leaves your fingertips free. Now when you bring your hand under the table, you scoop up the nickel on your knee and hold it with the penny.

And what do you hand your friend?

That's right, the penny and the nickel.

Which he thinks are the dime and the penny!

Now when you ask him to pass you the penny, he will slide you the nickel. He thinks that he is keeping the dime (because it's the smaller of the two coins), but it's the penny!

You simply drop the nickel onto your knee.

You say you will make the coins exchange places and slap the palmed dime down on the table. But he thinks that he is holding the dime. He brings his hand up and discovers that he is—amazingly—holding a penny.

# Behind the Magic

A lot of great magic depends on the wonder of misdirection. Here, the participant thinks that he is holding certain coins that he's seen. When the coins feel right, he doesn't question anything.

All the senses can be tricked. And, boy, are magicians glad about that!

# Five

## THE BEST NUMBER TRICKS EVER

*N*umbers are amazing things. They seem so real, but they can be used in countless tricks and illusions. Here is a collection of counting tricks, magical number arrays, and some amazing illusions and oddities—all involving numbers.

# 37

# TALKING DICE

## What You Need: 3 dice

## RATING: ♟ ♟

## The Illusion

Hand your friend three dice and then turn your back. Ask her to throw the dice on the table while you keep looking away.

Ask her to add up the three top faces. Then tell her to pick up any one die, any one at all, and add its bottom face to her total. Finally, have her roll this die one more time and add the new number it shows on top to the total.

You now turn around, to see the three dice, with no way of knowing which one was rolled again.

There's no way you could know the total, is there?

But you look down and, in a few moments, announce the correct total!

## Performing the Trick

To do this trick, just follow the steps above, instructing your friend to roll the dice and then select one to roll again. When you turn around, you look at the dice and act as if you are thinking hard. Total the faces showing and then merely add 7—and that will be your friend's total.

It works every time!

## Behind the Magic

The success of this trick depends on often-forgotten fact about dice: If you add any top and bottom face (or any opposing faces) they always add up to 7! So when your friend adds the bottom of one dice to its top, she is making a 7. When your friend rolls the die again, she thinks that there's no way you could know what the previous numbers were.

But you do! They added up to 7, as they always must.

Simply add 7 to the total on the table, and you have your friend's mystery total!

# 38
# MIXED-UP DICE

*What You Need: 1 die*

**RATING:** 🎩 🎩

## The Illusion

You hold a single die between your index finger and your thumb. You ask your friend to look at what numbers are showing on any opposing side of the die. For example, you show him that a 1 and a 6 are visible.

Then you ask him to take a look again, but now, there's a 3 on one side and a 4 on the other. The sides of the die have changed before your friend's eyes.

## Performing the Trick

Just like leopards, dice can't change their spots.

To do this trick, hold the die as described above, right between your index finger and your thumb. Let your friend see the 1 on one side, and the 6 on the opposite side.

Then you say that you can make the spots move, and you twist your hand to show your friend the 1 side again.

But as you twist your hand, you also *roll* the die a quarter of a turn, so a new side slips into place, a 3. Practice this move so the roll cannot be seen.

Your friend won't see the slight move. He'll see only your twist of the wrist. And of course, when you twist back to show the other face of the die, that too has changed.

## Behind the Magic

The key moment in this trick is combining the turning of your wrist with the little roll of the die. Done together, that roll is cannot be seen.

And you will be able to make the dots on dice seem to move.

# 39

# CALENDAR MAGIC

What You Need: a monthly calendar (any month will do), a pencil, and a calculator

RATING: ♟ ♟

## The Illusion

Here's a trick that requires a calculator unless you're *really* good in math!

You turn your back to your friend and have her mark a square on the calendar around 9 numbers (3 boxes by 3 boxes—see the illustration). Ask her to tell you the lowest number in that square . . . and then you will tell her the total of all the numbers in the square.

Unbelieving, she tells you the lowest number, you use the calculator briefly, and you announce the total of the square.

When she checks, she'll see that somehow you were able to give the total without seeing the square.

## Performing the Trick

Your friend marks a square, 3 boxes by 3 boxes, anywhere on the calendar. She tells you the lowest number in the square. Now comes the calculator magic. Whatever number your friend tells you, simply add 8 and then multiply that number by 9. The result will be the sum total of all 9 numbers in her square.

## Behind the Magic

Think about this one a second . . .

The lowest number will always be the one in the uppermost left-hand corner. The average number turns out to be 8 more. (That's why you add 8.) When you have the average of the 9 numbers, multiplying them by 9 gives you the total of all the boxes.

Got that?

To make this trick even more mystifying, rather than turning your back, ask your friend to blindfold you. Then you can either do the adding in your head or, even cooler, learn how to press the keys on the calculator without looking. That way you can say your calculator is magic. You ask the smallest number, pretend you're hitting some random keys, and there's the total.

Of course your friend may have to borrow the calculator to check!

# 40

## WATCH OUT!

*What You Need:* a watch or a
clock with hands (not digital!)

**RATING:** 🎩 🎩

### The Illusion

Ask your friend to think of any number on the watch face.
You then start tapping numbers on the watch face, telling
your friend to count your taps silently, starting with his original number. When he reaches 20, he should call out "Stop."

When he looks at the watch face, he sees that you are
touching his number!

### Performing the Trick

You do the trick exactly as described above. At the start, you
do tap the numbers on the watch randomly for the first 8 taps.
But you make sure that your *9th* tap lands on the 12.
Then tap backwards, counterclockwise, on the watch face
until your friend says Stop, and you will have ended on his
number!

## Behind the Magic

The trick here is almost no trick. When you tell your friend to count to 20 taps beginning with his number, he thinks that his number is hidden.

But he *tells* you when he reaches 20, which includes his number. Why do you start counting backwards from the *12* after the 8th tap? Because 8 and 12 also make 20. By counting backwards, you reveal the number he used to reach 20.

And the best part? Your friend will never see how you do it!

# 41

# THE TWO FOXES

## What You Need: 7 toothpicks

## RATING:

## The Illusion

You tell your friend a story about some chickens (five to be exact) and two foxes.

You take a toothpick in each hand to represent the foxes, and then each fox snatches a chicken—another toothpick—from the table.

Each fox goes in order, grabbing a chicken—but when you're done, one fox has only one chicken, while the other has four!

## Performing the Trick

Set the seven toothpicks on the table in front of your friend and say, indicating the center five, "These are five chickens."

Take a toothpick in each hand and say, "These are the two foxes, and they will snatch the chickens. Each fox will take a turn grabbing a chicken."

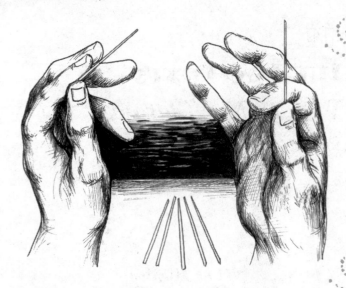

Starting with your *right* hand, grab a toothpick, then take one with your left hand, and so on until all the toothpicks are gone.

Then say, "But the foxes hear the farmer coming and let the chickens go!" Now begin replacing the toothpicks starting with the left hand.

Say: "But then the farmer leaves again, and the foxes once again steal the chickens." Start picking up the toothpicks, beginning with the *right* hand, taking one toothpick at a time.

When you're done, open your hands to show . . . five toothpicks in your right hand and only two in the left.

But wait, didn't each hand go in order? Shouldn't they have the same? How did that happen, your friend wonders.

You'll never tell!

## Behind the Magic

You make it appear as though each hand, each "fox," is picking up the same number of chickens.

But the trick is that you start picking up the toothpicks with your *right* hand . . . and then you put them back with your *left*. Since there are five toothpicks, an odd number, your right hand gets one more the first time the foxes snatch. Then, when you put them back, you *start* with your left—which leaves your left hand empty but your right hand holding two toothpicks.

When you pick up the toothpicks the second time—again starting with your right, which already has two toothpicks in it—you will end up with five toothpicks in your right hand and only two in your left.

Practice this trick so you get comfortable switching from hand to hand—and watch how confused the story of the foxes and the chickens makes your friend.

# DAVID COPPERFIELD
## Dreaming the Impossible

David Copperfield is one of today's greatest magicians, a performer whose massive illusions stun audiences around the world.

From his Broadway show, *Dreams and Nightmares*, to his two collections of magical stories, to his new theme restaurants in New York and Orlando, Copperfield has taken the world of magic to new heights.

Copperfield was born David Kotkin on September 16, 1956. He started performing in his hometown of Metuchen, New Jersey, when he was twelve, and it wasn't long before he became a member of the Society of American Magicians.

Now Copperfield performs the world over, on stage and on television. He specializes in illusions that defy belief. Copperfield has vanished the Statue of Liberty, walked through the Great Wall of China, and flown above the heads of countless audiences.

Copperfield pushes the limit of what a magician can do. "The secret," says the magician, "is to consider nothing impossible, then start treating possibilities as probabilities. If I am in the impossible business, and I am, then I want to go beyond impossible."

And yet the centerpiece of Copperfield's act is a bit of close-up magic, performed with an ordinary deck of cards, an illusion not unlike the ones you can learn from this book.

# Six

## VANISHINGS!

What can be more fun than making something disappear? Magicians are always making things go away—and here are some tricks that will make everything from coins to saltshakers *vanish!*

# 42

# POP GOES THE PENCIL

*What You Need:* an ordinary pencil and a cloth napkin

## RATING:

## The Illusion

You hold the pencil in your hand, sitting, and tell your friend that you will make it disappear. You then cover the pencil with the cloth napkin.

Then you say, "When I say 'Pop,' the pencil will disappear into thin air."

You wait a moment, the suspense unbearable, and then say: "Pop." You pull off the napkin to reveal that the pencil has, in fact, vanished.

Or has it?

## Performing the Trick

Practice this one a few times before you do it. The effect will be truly mysterious.

First, just as you cover the pencil, stick your index finger straight up. As you do that, let the pencil fall into your lap.

Now your friend thinks she sees the pencil covered by the napkin, but it's actually your finger.

When you pull the napkin off, just as quickly bring your finger down—and somehow the pencil has vanished before your friend's eyes.

## Behind the Magic

The more you practice this trick, the better it works. You want your finger to take the place of the pencil smoothly so there's no question that the pencil is—in fact—under the napkin.

# 43

# THE SALTSHAKER MYSTERY

*What You Need: a glass saltshaker filled with salt, a thick paper napkin, and a quarter*

## RATING:

## The Illusion

Here's an illusion in which you say you're going to make one thing disappear—and then you make something completely different vanish.

Tell your friend that you will make a quarter disappear. First you put the quarter on the table and then you take a saltshaker and cover it with a thick paper napkin.

Now you place the covered saltshaker over the quarter and say the magic words, "Coin Be Gone!"

You remove the saltshaker and . . . the quarter is still there. "Hmm," you say, "perhaps we'd better try that one again." So you cover the quarter again and you look up. Of course, you forgot to do something. You bring

QUARTER

your other hand down hard on the covered saltshaker, smashing it.

But now the saltshaker has vanished, an even more impressive feat than making a quarter disappear, wouldn't you say?

## Performing the Trick

Well, I'm sure you realize that *you* knew, all along, that you were really going to make the saltshaker disappear. But your friend doesn't suspect that at all. So what does he watch? Exactly, he watches the quarter.

You follow all the steps as described above. Put the quarter down, take the saltshaker, and cover it with a napkin.

Then cover the quarter with the covered saltshaker. And, of course, the quarter doesn't disappear.

But what happens next?

When you remove the covered saltshaker, you bring it back toward your edge of the table and, keeping the napkin in the shape of the saltshaker, let the saltshaker drop off the edge of the table.

The actual saltshaker falls into your lap while you return to the center of the table the napkin that you are holding in the *shape* of the saltshaker.

Now simply bring your other hand around to smash down on the saltshaker and your friend will see it vanish before his own eyes.

## Behind the Magic

If your friend was watching the saltshaker, he might notice that you brought it all the way to the edge of the table.

But he wasn't.

When you let it fall, your lap muffles any sound and—if you hold the napkin carefully—it seems as though you still have the saltshaker.

Oh—and here's an added twist to the trick. You smashed down on the saltshaker. So where did it go?

Reach under the table as though reaching down to the floor and bring the saltshaker back up.

"Sorry," you can say to your friend, "I accidentally knocked the saltshaker right through the table!"

# 44

# WHERE DID IT GO?–2

## What You Need: a pencil and a quarter

## RATING:

## The Illusion

You might think this trick about a disappearing quarter belongs in the coin-trick chapter of this book . . . but read on.

Start by telling your friend that you can do magic without any special kind of magic wand. In fact, you can even use a pencil.

You say you will make a quarter vanish before her eyes using nothing more than an ordinary pencil as a magic wand.

Place the quarter down on the table, then turn to the side and pick up your "magic wand," the pencil. Bring the pencil up and back toward your head once, twice, and then, on the third time, say, "Vanish"—but the quarter's still there!

"Gee, what happened?" you say.

Then you look into your hand and notice that the pencil has vanished!

But not really, as you laugh and show your friend that you cleverly stuck it behind your ear. You take the pencil out and wave it at the quarter—which now vanishes!

## Performing the Trick

As soon as you put the quarter on the table, turn to the side so your right ear is hidden (and ready to "catch" your pencil).

Then raise and lower the pencil, counting "One, two, three" as you bring it behind your head three times. But the third time you raise it, slip the pencil behind your ear.

Then when you lower your hand, it's empty. Ooops, you made the wrong thing disappear.

But then you let your friend in on the trick.

And why do you do this? After all, you know the Magician's Code.

Because when you turn to show her the pencil, she looks right at it—and she *totally* misses seeing you remove the quarter with your other hand. Now you take the pencil and quickly wave it to where the quarter used to be . . .

And you did what you set out to: You made the quarter disappear!

## Behind the Magic

The hardest part of this trick is getting the pencil behind your ear in a smooth, natural move so there's no interruption when you raise and lower it.

The other difficult part is smoothly grabbing the quarter with one hand while taking the pencil out from behind your ear. The moves must occur together.

Do it right, and you have a trick that has two vanishings—both done with an ordinary pencil!

# 45

# SEEING SPOTS

*What You Need:* a piece of cardboard approximately 6 by 8 inches and a marker

**RATING:** 🎩 🎩

## The Illusion

You hold a big piece of cardboard with dots in front of your friend. You ask him, "How many dots are on this card?"

He'll say—for the first side—that he sees 1 dot.

"Fine," you say, flipping the card over. "Now how many on this side?"

He'll look at it and say that he sees 6 dots.

"Exactly," you say. "But let's check that other side again, shall we?"

You flip it over and now he sees . . . 3 dots!

And the other side? Again, you flip the cardboard over and now he sees . . . 4 dots.

And by this time your friend is seeing spots.

# Performing the Trick

Before you're ready for your spotless performance, you'll need to make up a special card. Take your cardboard and a marker. Then make the card—in reality—have 2 dots on one side (side A), like this:

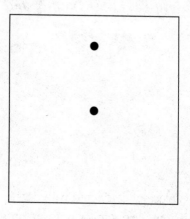

The other side, side B, has 5 dots arrayed like this:

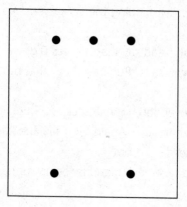

Now, armed with your special cards, you can dazzle your friend. First, show him side A, but with your hand and fingers hide the top dot. All he will see is that center dot, so he'll say that side A has 1 dot.

Now flip the card over, holding your fingers over the space where there is no dot. Your friend will say that there are 6 dots on the card, because he'll assume that there's a dot where you are holding the card.

Now flip the card back over to side A, but hold it right below the center dot, where a third dot might be—but isn't! Your friend will "see" that there are 3 dots on the card. Again, in his mind, he completes the pattern.

Flip over to side B, and hold the card so the top center dot is masked, and he will see . . . only 4 dots.

And it will seem to be quite a magical card you have!

## Behind the Magic

In this trick, the card does the fooling. But it will only work if you practice covering the spaces so that no one ever thinks there are no missing spots.

# 46

# THE MAGIC MATCHBOOK

## What You Need: 2 matchbooks (1 full, 1 empty) and a cup of tea in a saucer

## RATING: 🎩 🎩

### The Illusion

You know that you're not supposed to play with matches, right? This trick involves matchbooks—but we never light a single match.

You start with an empty matchbook and tell your friend a little-known fact about matchbooks. An empty matchbook always makes a full one appear beside it.

Always!

Hard to believe? You show your friend the empty matchbook, then take it back from her. You push the matchbook into your closed fist, wave your fist around, and open it to reveal . . . two matchbooks, but one has all its matches.

Just as you said!

## Performing the Trick

Well, an empty matchbook *will* always summon a full one—with a little help.

In this case, hidden behind your cup of tea is a full matchbook. When you hand your friend the empty matchbook to examine, with your other hand, you casually scoop up the full one hidden behind your cup.

When she gives you back the empty matchbook, it's a simple matter to stick it into your palm and wave your fist around. (Remember, make it dramatic—after all, you are a magician!)

Then open up your fist to show how the empty matchbook now has a full one beside it.

## Behind the Magic

(Or in this case, behind the teacup.)

The full matchbook isn't seen by your friend, who is sitting across from you. When you hand her the empty one to examine, you are—once again!—distracting her.

Meanwhile, while she was distracted, you have scooped up the full matchbook that's been waiting so patiently behind your cup.

Think how much trouble magicians would be in if people could watch two things at the same time!

# Seven

## Taking Magic Further

$\mathcal{C}$ongratulations! By now you know that you can do magic everywhere with some ordinary things. But you may be wondering where you go to get some cool tricks that *don't* use ordinary things.

And, yes, you can buy great tricks like the invisible deck. In that trick, a friend can turn an "invisible" card upside down in an "invisible" deck, and then you make that *deck* appear and guess what? His selected card is upside down.

Or how about a magic powder that you put into a cup of water and poof—the water disappears?

Or the newspaper that never falls apart even though you keep cutting it into strips.

Every magician uses tricks that involve special, magical objects, and there are a lot of places to get them. To expand your act with some extraordinary objects, here are some great sources for magic tricks that will let you order from a catalog or on-line on the Internet.

# Mail-Order Sources

## TANNEN'S MAGIC SHOP

Tannen's in New York is one of the oldest and most famous magic shops. Every professional magician knows about it, and many get tricks there. But though the store is located in New York, Tannen's is a great resource for you wherever you are. They publish a big catalog with thousands of great tricks that you can order. They also publish a regular newsletter with new tricks you can buy. Tannen's even has a summer camp for kids who want to learn how to become performing magicians and put on shows.

You can contact Tannen's to request information about their big catalog and to be put on their mailing list.

**TANNEN'S
24 WEST 25TH STREET
NEW YORK, NY 10010
212-929-4500 (1-800-72-MAGIC)**

Tannen's new website is www.tannenmagic.com. There are lots of great tricks available.

## HANK LEES MAGIC FACTORY

Hank Lees Magic Factory is a great mail resource for tricks, and it also has a big catalog that will get you itchy to buy some very cool tricks. You can order coin tricks, card tricks, mental magic, and even big tricks for stage magic.

Contact them at their toll-free hot line:
1-800-874-7400

Their fax number is 617-395-2034, and you can email them at MagicFact@aol.com from your computer.

## Magic on the Internet

A great way to find magic tricks and information about your favorite magicians in on-line, on the Internet. You can also find places to talk about magic and ask questions.

It used to be that if you didn't live close to a magic shop or know a magician personally, it was pretty hard to learn any new tricks.

The Internet has changed all that. The "Net" is exploding with great magic sites. You'll find on-line shops selling classic tricks and brand-new illusions. You can shop a "virtual catalog" and see some really great tricks.

Not only that, there are sites devoted to great magicians like Houdini and David Copperfield, as well as dozens of other performing magicians.

Are there any tricks? Yes, most of the sites listed below feature great on-line magic tricks that are amazing. Other sites show you how to perform classic illusions. There's an entire world of magic awaiting you on-line.

*A few words of warning.* Whenever you go surfing for cool sites, it's important to make sure your parents know where you are going. It's a big world on the Net, and you don't want to get lost. Some sites are selling tricks—which is fine—but if you want to buy something, that's the time to make sure Mom or Dad is right next to you to do the actual ordering.

A good general rule is that you should never give anyone on-line any of your personal information, like your full name, address, or phone number.

Okay? Now you're all set to experience the world of magic on the Net. There are hundreds of magic sites. I've selected a few to get you started that will make hours, if not days, disappear!

## MAGICAL SITES

### THE WEB OF MAGIC

www.websmart.com/cgi-data/magic1.html

Here's a great place to start looking for everything magical on the Web. From here you can jump to some cool sites like the Balloon Archives (all balloon magic!), the College of Magic, the Conjuring Cabaret (filled with interesting tricks for sale), the Magic Castle (a club for professional magicians only), the Magic Place (for kids who do magic), and many others, including sites about carnival magic and the great magicians like Houdini.

### THE ALL MAGIC GUIDE

www.allmagic.com/allmagicguide/

This great magic site features not only interviews and tricks but also a magic calendar listing magicians performing in the United States, a guide to dozens of dealers who sell magic tricks, and special events, including live chats with famous magicians about "Stage Secrets." You'll find a lot of places that can send you magic catalogs—more than you ever dreamed.

## THE MAGIC PAGE

www.daimi.aau.dk/~zytnia/eg.html

This giant page is based in Denmark and features enough magical information and links to keep you busy for a long time. There are stories and articles about magic in the movies and TV, and news of upcoming magic shows.

But the most fun is the giant listing of magicians who have pages on the Internet, dealers selling tricks, and people who simply want to do magic on the Net.

This page also has links to major magicians such as Penn & Teller and James Randi.

There are a lot of magic companies listed, but you'll also find lots of pages with free tricks for you to learn—some of them very cool indeed.

## THE SECOND DEAL

www.theseconddeal.com

This is a site for magicians only. To enter you'll have to answer some questions about tricks, most of which you should be able to answer from the tricks in this book. And what will you find once you're inside the Second Deal site?

Once you're in, you'll get lots of behind-the-scenes information about tricks and magicians, as well as links to other great magic sites. Since this is a site for performing magicians, the links are among the best.

## THE OFFICIAL DAVID COPPERFIELD SITE

www.dcopperfield.com/cgi-bin/copper.cgi

This is the official Copperfield site, loaded with information about Copperfield's performance dates and locations, as well as news about the new magic restaurants he's opened in New York and Orlando. There are chats about magic, a message board, and even a magic game—Deathsaw Challenge!

## MAGIC CARD TRICK

www.rit.edu/~dmm4971/trick1.html

The listing of sites wouldn't be complete without one great Internet card trick. Go to this page to check out a great card illusion from Doug Mattingly that you can do right over the Internet! Can you figure out how it's done?

## THE OFFICIAL PENN & TELLER SITE

www.sincity.com/penn-n-teller/magic.html

Penn & Teller enjoy getting weird in their magic act, and their site gives you news of their upcoming appearances. Like their show, the site is loaded with weirdness.

## MAGICAL SECRETS

www.magical.com/links.html

Here's probably the most comprehensive list of magic sites, shops, clubs, newsletters, and on-line illusions on the Internet. Best of all, there's even a special magic-trick search engine so you can hunt down specific tricks you may have seen.

# INDEX

# About the Author

MATTHEW J. COSTELLO is the author of fifteen novels and numerous nonfiction articles and books. He wrote the script for Virgin Interactive's *The 7th Guest,* which remains the best-selling CD-ROM interactive drama of all time (more than 2,000,000 copies sold). Recently, Costello helped develop for the Disney Channel *ZoogDisney,* a new on-air/on-line bloc of programs designed to merge the worlds of TV and the computer.